AUGUSTE COMTE
MEMORIAL TRUST LECTURE

No. 3

War and
Industrial Society

BY

RAYMOND ARON

Litt.D., Chevalier de la Légion d'Honneur

Professor of Sociology
in the University of Paris

TRANSLATED BY MARY BOTTOMORE

Delivered on 24 OCTOBER 1957
at the London School of Economics
and Political Science

GREENWOOD PRESS, PUBLISHERS
WESTPORT, CONNECTICUT

Library of Congress Cataloging in Publication Data

Aron, Raymond, 1905-
  War and industrial society.

    Reprint of the 1958 ed. published by the Oxford Uni-
versity Press, London, which was issued as no. 3 of the
series: Auguste Comte memorial trust lecture.
    1. War and society--Addresses, essays, lectures.
I. Title. II. Series: Auguste Comte memorial trust
lecture ; no. 3.
[HM36.5.A7 1980]   303.6'6   80-19002
ISBN 0-313-22512-5 (lib. bdg.)

Reprinted with the permission of The London School of
Economics and Political Science.

Reprinted in 1980 by Greenwood Press
A division of Congressional Information Service, Inc.
88 Post Road West, Westport, Connecticut 06881

Printed in the United States of America

10 9 8 7 6 5 4 3 2 1

WAR AND INDUSTRIAL SOCIETY

We are too much obsessed by the twentieth century to spend time in speculating about the twenty-first. Long-range historical predictions have gone out of fashion. George Orwell's portrait of 1984 depicted too faithfully the last years of Stalinism to have any great value as an anticipation. Atomic weapons seem to confront us with a simple choice between permanent peace and universal suicide; and they are as discouraging to pacifist dreams as to militaristic nightmares. The Third Reich, instituted for a thousand years, collapsed in ruins at the end of twelve years; the Soviet régime, founded by revolutionaries in the name of Western humanism and the classless society, ended in the totalitarianism which Mr. Kruschev described in the style of *Ubu Roi* at the Twentieth Congress of the Bolshevik Party. Mankind's intimate and tragic experience of these two millenial realms is such that political aspirations are unlikely, in the immediate future, to take again the form of a secular religion.

The thinkers of last century had a stronger feeling of living in a period of transition, and they did not hesitate to make prophecies whose boldness and dogmatism astound us. I am reminded of the remark of an historian of religion on the subject of Roman Catholicism: 'The wind of the coming century will scatter its ashes.' Equally imprudent today appears the assurance with which Auguste Comte wrote in 1842: 'At last the time has come when serious and lasting war must disappear completely among the human élite' (*Cours de philosophie positive*, t. vi, lect. 57, p. 239). In that lecture Comte heralded the approach of peace, and asserted the absolute incompatibility between the military spirit and industrial society. It seemed to me that there could be no worthier tribute to the memory of a great man than a consideration of one of his mistakes. In the history of thought errors are often more instructive than truths; the latter become platitudes and are integrated into the general body of knowledge, while the former, when they are not forgotten, remain isolated and open to investigation. They call for an explanation and bear witness to the limitation of even the greatest intellects.

I

In the first half of last century sociologists and philosophers who reflected upon the course of history were all struck by the development of industrial society, that is, by the concurrent processes of construction of factories, extension of the use of machinery, concentration of the working class in towns, increase in world population, and the drift to the towns of men who had become useless in the countryside. These phenomena, which we a hundred years later can see in truer perspective than contemporaries were able to do, provoked diverse attitudes and were judged in contradictory ways.

The optimists marvelled at the progress of science and technology and the ever-increasing productive capacity, and they visualized an era of prosperity and peace resulting from the extension of an exchange economy. The pessimists drew attention to the misery of the working class and to the unequal distribution of wealth produced in common. Some of them doubted whether the workers' standard of living could ever rise appreciably; a rise in wages would encourage an increase in population which would soon reduce them again.

During this period there emerged the great doctrines whose impact dominated ideological controversies, and to some extent scientific thought itself, up to the war of 1939. Does the system of free enterprise and competition allow an indefinite expansion of production, or is it doomed to periodic crises and indeed condemned sooner or later to a total paralysis which will render inevitable the emergence of a new system? Will the incontestable growth in the means of production lead to an era of abundance, or will the increase in wealth merely lead to a growth of population, so that the achievements of human ingenuity benefit only a minority?

Among the doctrines formulated and diffused in this period (which we might call the first phase of industrialization), the most famous is that of Marx, which combines optimism and pessimism in a striking manner. Optimism, perhaps excessive, about the contribution of capitalism to powers of production is allied with pessimism, certainly excessive, about the condition of the masses in an economy based upon private property and competition. Unbounded optimism about the fate of humanity after the liberating revolution, accompanies a pessimistic view, not yet justified, of the ability of capitalism to overcome its own contradictions. Elsewhere I have characterized Marxism as 'catastrophic optimism', in order to indicate one of the unique features which has contributed so much to its propaganda value. With regard to industrial civilization itself, Marx shares the confidence of the optimistic school, and perhaps even carries it further; with regard to the future of capitalism and the fate of the masses under this system, he shares the fears of the pessimistic school. The industrial reserve army will prevent wages from rising, crises will become more and more violent, the class struggle will become more intense. History must pass through the purgatory of civil war before attaining the paradise of plenty and a humanity reconciled with itself thanks to its victory over nature.

These doctrinal controversies have not entirely disappeared in the mid-twentieth century. One still finds, in the West, fanatical supporters of planning or of the market mechanism, economists and sociologists who place all their hopes in one system and all their fears in the other. But on the whole, the ideological response has been gradually replaced by scientific analysis. It has been possible to distinguish the phenomena common to the initial stages of industrialization, whatever the régime, to note the variations of these phenomena according to the methods used, and to attempt a comparison of the relative cost of industrialization in different places. Instead of predicting the stability, rise, or fall of wage-levels with the development of productive forces, we measure the rate of economic growth necessary to balance or surpass the growth of population. Global prophecies are replaced by correlations and by probability calculations for a particular country or a particular situation.

The nineteenth-century predictions concerning peace and war also oscillated between optimism and pessimism. But the two schools disagreed less about the evolution of industrial society itself than about the place of industrial society in world history and the significance of industrialism in modern civilization. The optimistic school, to which Auguste Comte and (with some qualifications) Herbert Spencer belonged, saw history as a unilinear movement from one type of society to another; military society and industrial society represented two fundamentally different types of social organization. The predominance of the second type would diminish warfare, which is essentially connected with the predominance of the first. On the other hand, the pessimistic school, represented by Nietzsche, Burckhardt, and Spengler (who wrote in the twentieth century but before the outbreak of 1914), saw in so-called industrial societies only another version of the urban societies, the popular mass civilizations, whose rise in antiquity was marked by the civil wars at the end of the Roman Republic. When Nietzsche predicted that the twentieth century would be one of great wars it seems to me that his prescience was based on two observations: that urban mass civilizations are bellicose and not pacific, and that the spread of Western civilization over the globe would offer the contending great powers an immense prize—world domination.

If this analysis is correct, the contrast between the two schools, that which foresees peace and that which predicts great wars, derives from a more profound disagreement—that between a progressive and a cyclical conception of history. Industrial society, in Auguste Comte's opinion, gave promise of peace because it was the culmination of a unique development. Industrial society was going to be the scene of one of the greatest wars in history, according to Spengler, because the concentration of the masses in towns, the rule of money, the disintegration of communities based on kinship, and the domination of demagogues and plutocrats made inevitable clashes between the different wills to power, concealed by changing ideologies.

If this is so, the problem of the bellicose or pacific nature of industrial societies has certainly not been resolved by the tragic experiences of the first half of the twentieth century. In economic matters the past half-century, it seems to me, has strengthened the case of those who take a middle position. Science and industry have upset the organization of human groups and have not entirely justified either optimism (capitalist or socialist) or pessimism, still less catastrophic optimism. But we now know approximately the circumstances in which societies can take advantage of knowledge and technique to provide better material conditions for a growing proportion of people. We do not know if and when the whole of humanity will succeed in creating these conditions.

With regard to peace and war, the middle position seems excluded by the existence of atomic weapons. If the efficiency of these weapons is as great as scientists say, would not a single war, carried out with all the available weapons, destroy at one blow civilization as we know it? And if the optimists are not absolutely right, will not the pessimists be vindicated by events or even appear to have been insufficiently pessimistic?

Since the question as to whether industrial civilizations are inherently pacific remains unanswered, it is worthwhile to examine more closely the proofs of their pacific character which were offered a century ago by Auguste Comte, and to test these proofs by the historical events of the period between Comte and ourselves.

The fundamental idea in Auguste Comte's theory—the radical opposition between the military spirit and the industrial spirit— was a commonplace in the first half of last century. It was first formulated by Saint-Simon and was suggested by the obvious changes in Western societies. Work was becoming the principal activity of the immense majority of men, and the activity which pre-eminently conferred wealth, power, and prestige. From that time the real élite in society was composed of bankers, industrialists, engineers, and scientists, not of aristocrats. But the hierarchy of values which is established by the ruling class must surely make an impression upon society as a whole and upon the course of social development. In the view of bankers, industrialists, and engineers, wars are an anachronism, a survival of former times. They squander wealth, whereas the function of work is to create it, and the major concern of those who direct the collective labour of society is to prevent waste and encourage creative activity.

This fundamental antithesis of military civilization and the civilization of labour, of the spirit of conquest and the spirit of industry, was projected by Comte into history, the former into antiquity and the latter into modern times. In antiquity, work was the duty of slaves, and free men were available for war. The primitive aversion from a life of labour made the use of force unavoidable in the first phase of man's education. The unification of the ancient world by a conquering empire was the inevitable outcome of the warlike ardour of free men. 'The primitive institution of permanent slave labour had, by its very nature, a two-fold aim; on the one hand, to allow military activity a sufficient growth to accomplish properly its first great mission in the process of social evolution, and on the other hand, to establish the only general means of education which, by an invincible pressure, could overcome the radical antipathy felt by most men at first for the habit of regular work.'[1] 'The first great mission' was the expansion of human societies. 'There was no other means, in the early stages, to bring about the indispensable expansion of human society, and to restrain within society, a sterile war-like ardour incompatible with an adequate growth of productive work, except the gradual incorporation of civilised populations into one conquering nation' (vi. 57, p. 287).

In the ancient world, therefore, work was subordinate to war, first, because the slave was constrained by force, and thus by the warrior, secondly, because the latter performed the essential function of extending human groups by conquest, and finally, as a result of the Roman Empire. But Comte argues—and here he is in agreement with Hegel's *Phenomenology of Mind*—that a complete reversal occurred between antiquity and modern times. Then, labour was subordinate to war; the epochs of modern times are stages in the subordination of war to labour. In the first phase, industrial society developed purely spontaneously, 'helped only by fortunate natural alliances with various ancient powers' (ibid., p. 80). In the succeeding phase, industry was favoured as an indispensable means to military supremacy. In the third phase, industrial development was 'finally established as a permanent goal of European politics which nevertheless has regularly made use of war' (p. 80). First, industry in the service of war, then war in the service of industry, and the final synthesis in the ultimate form of society will be peace through industry.

Like Spencer and the other optimists Auguste Comte saw

[1] *Cours de philosophie positive*, vol. vi, lect. 56, p. 23.

clearly that industry could be used as an instrument of the will to power and as a tool of political ambition. We have still to inquire why he regarded these two phases, industry subordinate to the military spirit and militarism utilized to further industrial prosperity, as transitory. After all, the Marxist theory of imperialism means regarding this second phase as inescapable, at least while capitalism itself endures. As to the first phase, that of industry in the service of war, the Spengler school of pessimists believes this to be coextensive with industrial civilization, a characteristic of the Faustian west. What are the arguments, general and historical, explicit and implicit, with which Comte supports his view?

The argument, at once implicit and fundamental, derives from the way in which industry and the industrial spirit are defined. Comte did not use the word industry in its narrow sense to distinguish it from agriculture and commerce; industry includes agriculture, factory production, commerce, and finance. It is defined, first and foremost, by regular, free labour. Industrial solidarity is 'essentially founded on universal emancipation' (p. 71). It puts an end to the régime of classes and hereditary occupations, and encourages everyone to choose his work according to his ability or inclination. In other words, industrialization as interpreted by Comte is primarily defined not by the development of productive forces or the use of machinery but by the substitution of labour (or action on nature) for war as the predominant activity, and by the substitution of liberty for slavery or serfdom. This essential incompatibility does not, however, justify any historical prediction (unless associated with the extremely optimistic view that what is useless will disappear and that what has no function will not be produced). Why, then, did Comte believe that the wars of earlier stages will not be repeated?

In the third phase there was 'a final series of wars, the commercial wars, in which the military spirit tended, at first spontaneously and soon systematically, to subordinate itself to the formerly inferior industrial spirit, in order to retain a permanent active role, and thereafter attempted to integrate itself into the new social economy by demonstrating its special ability either to conquer useful trading centres for all nations or to destroy their principal sources of dangerous foreign competition' (p. 73). In short, why should we suppose that the period of imperialist wars (in Lenin's sense) has come to an end?

Wars of this type—colonial wars and wars in the service of the national economy—took place in the eighteenth century. But, according to Comte, the colonial régime was now in complete decline, 'the separation of the American colonies was bringing about its destruction in such a way as to prevent any serious renewal of the major wars to which it had previously given rise' (p. 236). Comte acknowledged that England was exceptional in enjoying, with its empire, a unique prosperity. But he urged the other nations of the European Republic not to take offence at the anomaly 'which corresponded to needs and abilities which could not exist elsewhere to the same degree'.

The wars of the Revolution and the Empire must have aroused anxiety in the mind of the founder of Positivism. But he saw in them the confirmation of the opposition between modern social relations and the military spirit, because it was 'for the temporary re-establishment of a régime radically antipathetic to the corresponding social milieu' that Napoleon plunged into 'vast military activities'. Far from renewing the work of the Roman Republic or of Charlemagne, the Emperor misunderstood the necessities of history, and he stimulated 'nations to join the king in repulsing foreign invasion, and thus destroyed the sympathy and admiration that our revolutionary initiative and popular defence had everywhere aroused among our western fellow citizens' (p. 215).

This 'tremendous warlike aberration' is henceforth impossible 'since ideological wars, which alone remain conceivable, have been radically checked by the growth of revolutionary activity in the West. This has become for Europe today an assurance of temporary peace by continuously occupying all the attention of governments and all the activity of their numerous armies to prevent internal disturbance' (p. 237).

Beyond this peace which fear of the people and the growth of revolutionary activity must impose on governments, 'the true intellectual reorganization' will intervene to establish genuine peace.

Only one kind of war remains conceivable, that which aims 'to establish directly, in the ultimate interest of universal civilization, the material preponderance of more advanced over less advanced populations' (p. 237). Such a tendency, which Comte resolutely condemned, might 'cause the mutual oppression of nations' and finally 'precipitate various cities upon one another according to their unequal social progress' (p. 238). With undaunted optimism, Comte tries to dispel 'all irrational anxiety', puts his confidence in 'the instinct characteristic of modern social relations', and refuses to envisage that this will to conquest, which justifies itself by the superiority of the white race, could become 'a new source of general war entirely incompatible with the most steadfast inclinations of all civilized populations' (p. 238).

The above quotations show that, if Comte believed that the time of peace had come for the élite of humanity, it was not because he failed to observe the possible causes of war in his time: *colonial wars* in which overseas territories conquered by European nations would be the stake, and which had occupied the eighteenth century, and *ideological wars* whose justification would be the superiority of European nations and which would culminate in the extension of colonial slavery in the guise of spreading civilization. Comte recognized the possibility and even the danger of all the kinds of war which have occupied the years since the positivist doctrine foretold the coming of peace. But he dispelled 'the irrational anxiety' and refused to envisage the return of the 'aberrations' because his whole interpretation of history was bound up with two ideas; first, the radical opposition between military society and industrial society, and secondly, the inevitable disappearance of phenomena not in accord with the spirit of the time. Comte could not envisage the case of a society which would destroy itself by its own folly, and he could not admit the hypothesis of a phenomenon attaining its extreme form at the point where it had lost all its usefulness. Moreover, he was led to discover a proof of the pacifism of European societies in facts which apparently suggested a contrary interpretation.

Was conscription becoming not a revolutionary improvisation but a permanent institution? Comte was sure that it provided proof of the anti-militarist feelings of modern populations. There are still volunteer officers but not volunteer soldiers. The military profession is losing its specialization and prestige, and civilians in uniform wait for their freedom and rebel increasingly against 'the temporary burden' (p. 239). The maintenance of great armies in peace-time? They are only 'great political police forces', the 'last function of order allotted to the military body at a time when true warfare is about to disappear for ever' (p. 241). In the same way, the revolutionary and imperial crisis has shown that 'the popular will' is sufficient to assure the success of a defensive action and that the most skilful tactics, if not supported by such a purpose, will ultimately fail. Henceforth there is no need to rely on the warlike virtues or to be obsessed by military successes.

Paradoxically enough, Comte finds the best proof of this fundamental pacifism of industrial society in the inferiority of the weapons used in comparison with those that are possible. 'It is clear that the means of warfare are infinitely inferior to the powerful and rapid increase in the stock of destructive machinery that our knowledge and resources would permit if modern nations could ever experience, in exceptional circumstances, even a temporary stimulus similar to that which moved the whole of the ancient world' (p. 57).

In fact, Comte was not mistaken on this last point. The 'exceptional circumstances' of 1914–18 subjected Europeans to a 'temporary stimulus'. Armoured vehicles and aircraft emerged transformed from these 'exceptional circumstances'. The Second World War which began with the weapons of 1918, ended with the first two atomic bombs. The apparatus of destruction had, as Comte would have said, undergone a 'powerful increase'.

II

Western society, which was to have guided humanity by way of peace to its final destination, was the birthplace and nursery, but also the victim, of the great wars of the twentieth century which pessimistic observers had seen looming on the horizon. The only question worthy of examination concerns the nature of these modern wars: are they colonial wars, ideological wars, or imperialist wars?

In my view, the First World War belongs to none of these

categories: it is characterized less by its immediate causes or its explicit purposes than by its extent and the stakes involved. It affected *all* the political units inside *one* system of relations between sovereign states. Let us call it, for want of a better term, a war of *hegemony*,[1] hegemony being, if not the conscious motive, at any rate the inevitable consequence of the victory of at least one of the states or groups. The victory of the Central Powers would have established the hegemony of Germany over Europe. The victory of Athens in the fifth century B.C. would have given domination of the whole Greek world to the city of Pericles. The victory of the Western nations resulted in the restoration, at least temporarily, of the 'liberties' of the European states, as that of Sparta restored the liberties of the Greek cities.

Comte declared that clashes between European nations had become impossible,[2] yet such conflicts have filled the first half of the twentieth century. He imagined the nations of Europe (England, Germany, Italy, Spain, and France) uniting into one Western republic and by their example guiding the rest of humanity without any wish to conquer it by force of arms. How different the reality has been from these prophecies, and how obvious it now seems that the prophecies were wiser and more in accord with the interests of everybody than were the actual events. A Franco-German war was necessary in order that the German nation should be united. In the last quarter of the nineteenth century the nations of Europe chose the way which the founder of positivism had advised against; they assumed 'the white man's burden'; they spread civilization by conquest and invoked their superiority to justify their dominance. Overseas possessions were probably not the cause, but inevitably they seemed one of the stakes in the conflicts between the metropolitan states. All the European nations were swept along by the development of industrial civilization, but while the conflict could not be reduced to the antithesis of the *ancien régime* and the revolution, neither were the European nations unified under the banner of a single philosophy. The 'ideologies' of the Euro-

---

[1] Such wars could also be called *wars of equilibrium* if they were defined with reference to the side which is on the defensive.

[2] Because of 'universal internal agitation'.

pean nations remained diverse enough, not to cause national clashes, but to aggravate them. No one in England or France would have thought of beginning a war in order to overthrow the absolutist régimes (which were in fact limited) of Imperial Germany or Austria-Hungary. But once war was declared, democracy could be extolled against absolutism.

If the 'national clashes', which Comte declared impossible, nevertheless took place, then those factors which tended to extend wars, which the pacifism of industrial society should have prevented, would come into operation. If conscript armies ceased to be police forces, they would provide the war lords with an almost inexhaustible human material (if one may use this abominable term). If the entrepreneurs, engineers, and scientists began to devote their talents to the apparatus of destruction instead of the instruments of production, what diabolical marvels they could pour out from the factories and machines.

Why did the European nations embark in 1914 upon a war of hegemony? The question has been hotly discussed because, perhaps for the first time in history, the belligerents had a vague sentiment that war itself was absurd and ruinous to their common civilization, and that those who began it were therefore criminals. The search for these war criminals was unrewarding because in fact nobody had wanted a war of this kind—cataclysmic, all-devouring, and increasingly devoid of purpose as it developed. Was the chief fault committed by those who wanted to teach a lesson to little Serbia or by those who had brought into operation the system of alliances and thus generalized the conflict? Or should the blame be distributed according to the war aims of the two sides? In that case, whatever treaty terms a victorious Germany would have dictated, she was the most guilty (like Athens in the Peloponnesian War) because in the event of victory she would have become the dominant power.

The European nations had not been pacified by industrialism. In August 1914 they were rich and prosperous, and no revolutionary agitation seriously threatened them. Amidst popular enthusiasm they entered upon a war which they probably imagined would be like so many others in the past. Nationalist conflicts in South-eastern Europe and Austro-Russian rivalry in the Balkans were the immediate causes of the outbreak. But this would have been impossible if, after a half-century of peace in Europe, the nations had not retained intact their warlike fervour and had not regarded their independence, as against the dictatorship of a single power, as a benefit worthy of the greatest sacrifices. Societies whose armies are made up of civilians in uniform are not necessarily peace-loving.

The First World War, which originated in a minor diplomatic conflict, was generalized by the system of alliances and assumed gigantic proportions as a result of conscription and the resources of industry. It was also the cause of the Second World War, because the victors were unwilling to impose their own hegemony and were unable to establish a real equilibrium. The U.S.A., which had given the *coup de grâce* to the Central Powers, retired from the game. Great Britain, having failed to recover its prosperity and being uncertain of the morality of the Versailles Treaty, left France to maintain equilibrium. And equilibrium could only be maintained, against the interests of the two great continental powers, Russia and Germany, by the permanent disarmament of Germany.

The second war of this century, even more vast than the first, was not essentially a war of hegemony. It was an ideological war, since the two sides invoked conflicting ideologies, and it was also an imperialist war, since Hitler's Germany aimed not perhaps at extending its conquests beyond Europe but at subjecting the other European nations to the kind of rule which these same nations had imposed overseas upon the so-called inferior or less advanced populations.

The inevitable result of what Comte would probably have called a 'temporary and tragic aberration' was the general ruin of those nations which should have constituted the Western republic and which live today, reconciled but not united, under the protection of the American Republic.

This interpretation of the last half-century may perhaps be summarized as follows: European politics have developed in the twentieth century in accordance with precedent and tradition, as though industrial civilization had brought nothing new. The European nations were unable either to unite in a single state or to live peacefully together as sovereign states united in the same civilization. Germany, the last to achieve national unity, was tempted in her turn by dreams of empire. Like Spain and France before her, and in spite of industrialism, she plunged or was drawn into the struggle for hegemony.

Whatever the uniqueness of the present state of affairs, the first half of the twentieth century favours the thesis of the pessimists who expected from the future nothing that they had not known in the past. Antiquity gave us the spectacle of a war to the death between sovereign states of the same civilization, fought all the more bitterly because the states were so close to each other. Thucydides summed up these events admirably in the phrase: κτῆμα ἐς ἀεί.

A number of thinkers—among them Veblen, Schumpeter, and the Marxists—have tried to explain this 'tragic aberration' in such a way as to maintain the pacific character of industrial societies.

It has hardly been noticed, in fact, but it seems to me incontestable, that Veblen's and Schumpeter's interpretations of imperialism are inspired by Positivism. Modern societies would be more prone to conquest and war, the more numerous the institutional and moral survivals of the feudal or aristocratic spirit. Germany and Japan have been the disturbing elements of this century because industrial society developed there in a framework inherited from the *ancien régime* and under the direction of a managerial class loyal to military values. Veblen, as is well known, predicted the flowering of Japanese imperialism as we in fact experienced it in the Asian co-prosperity sphere.

Undoubtedly the comparison is striking. Germany and Japan were the only two great industrial powers of our time governed by an aristocracy whose ethic and social attitudes dated from the pre-industrial period. The reformers of the Meiji era understood (as Chinese civil servants and scholars refused to understand) that it was necessary to adopt the industrial system of the West in order to preserve the independence and greatness of the empire. These reformers came from the class of nobles which had been subject to the authority of the Shogun during the two centuries of the Tokugawa period but which had not been destroyed. From this class were recruited the civil servants, teachers, business leaders, and officers who learned from the West and accomplished the most remarkable work of modernization of a non-Western country that we have seen up to the present time. The reformers did not stop at adopting weapons and factories, or even the organization of armies and factories; they also introduced universal compulsory education, changed the legal system to adapt it to the needs of a modern economy, created universities of a Western type, and in short, tried to give to the various classes of the nation the intellectual training required by economic development.

This process of Westernization was excluded from only two spheres, that which concerned the position of the family, children's education, and the traditional organization of personal relations, and that which concerned the emperor, as the source of power and descendant of the gods. The traditionalistic restoration of Shintoism seemed to the modernists to provide a counterweight to technical Westernization. Japan retained intact its ancestral spirit and culture in the age of submarines, skyscrapers, and internal combustion engines.

This combination of an industrial society and an *ancien régime*, to use the language of Comte, culminated in the catastrophe of 1945, after half a century of brilliant and uninterrupted success.

The reformers had created industry to preserve Japan's independence. The power which resulted inspired them with the desire to conquer. The easy victories over China and Korea followed by the resounding success over Russia gave them an exaggerated idea of their country's resources. Meanwhile, the increase of population fostered by governments anxious to acquire the force of numbers, had reached such a point that their agriculture, in spite of exceptionally rapid progress, could no longer feed all the Japanese. The export of manufactured goods really became a matter of life and death. Tens of millions of people lived by industrial work and this required the import of raw materials which could only be financed by the export of manufactured products. Impediments to export appeared as so many threats to the very existence of the Empire of the Rising Sun.

The conquest of territory in the islands or on the continent was not the only way of solving the problem of the Japanese economy. The protection of the flag is not indispensable for commercial expansion, and trade is possible without the acquisition of sovereignty. A co-prosperity area would have been conceivable without domination by the stronger power and probably even without a common currency. Conquest appeared to some members of the ruling class as a means of balancing the budget, and of feeding a growing population, but the increase of population had been encouraged. The conquest of Formosa and of Korea had preceded the alleged need for raw materials and trade outlets.

In seventy years, from 1870 to 1940, Japan lived through the equivalent of four centuries of European history as seen by Comte: it began by setting up industry to strengthen its army, like the states of Europe in the fifteenth and sixteenth centuries; afterwards it put its army at the service of the Asian co-prosperity sphere, thus reviving the colonial enterprises of eighteenth-century Europe. Since the defeat, it has been cured of these two compounds of the military spirit and the industrial spirit, which were the source of war for four centuries in Europe and for seventy years in Asia.

Japanese imperialism can be explained fairly simply in the framework and within the concepts of Comte's theory. In relation to Japan's past it seems a mystery. Japanese militarism had been chiefly feudal in spirit, 'defensive militarism' to use Comte's term. Unification under the authority of the Shoguns had condemned the class of nobles to internal and external peace. The policy of isolation, population stability, and the maintenance of the social hierarchy all tended, during the Tokugawa period, towards the permanence of order in a closed society. From the time of the Meiji era all was movement: increase of population, economic growth, increase of territory and of national strength. Having entered into competition with the West, Japan wanted to be first. The traditional militarism, armed by modern industry in an expanding universe, was transformed into the ambition to conquer. The European nations were great in proportion to their colonies. Japan wanted to compete and to surpass them. Thus the foolish decision of 1941, without appearing inevitable, be-

comes intelligible. Japan, unable to conquer the vast area and
the masses of China, attacked the world's greatest industrial
power.

The spirit of the *ancien régime* was certainly not the only force
in the formation of modern Germany. She has passed through all
the characteristic stages of European history, has played an important part in all Western intellectual movements, and has experienced all the social classes and all the industrial activities
characteristic of Western civilization. Nevertheless, Imperial
Germany differed profoundly from the Western democracies.
After the defeat of 1848 the liberal *bourgeoisie* was eliminated
from the political scene and left the principal role to the civil
servants and Prussian officers. German unity was achieved by
Prussia's military victories, not by deliberative assemblies and
popular enthusiasm. Up to 1914 the Prussian electors voted by
estates, not by universal suffrage; the monarchy was constitutional, not parliamentary. The system of values and the way of
thinking characteristic of the governing class were not so much
those of an industrial or commercial *bourgeoisie* as those of aristocratic functionaries, civil servants, and officers.

The facts which Veblen and Schumpeter can quote in support
of their theory are not open to doubt. The survivals of the *ancien
régime* were stronger in Germany and Japan than in Great Britain
or France. In both countries there was this combination of a
property-owning class and a military caste which can be regarded
as the chief cause of imperialism.

The article published by Veblen in 1915, 'The Opportunity of
Japan',[1] in retrospect seems prophetic:

It is in this unique combination of a high wrought spirit of feudalistic
fealty and chivalric honour with the material efficiency given by the
modern technology that the strength of the Japanese nation lies. In this
respect—in being able anachronistically to combine the use of modern
technical ways and means with the mediaeval spirit of servile solidarity
—the position of the Japanese government is not unique except in the
eminent degree of its successful operation. The several governments
of Europe are also, and with a varying measure of success, endeavor-
ing similarly to exploit the modern state of the industrial arts by

[1] Reproduced in *Essays in Our Changing Order*, New York, 1934.

recourse to the servile patriotism of the common man, and for the purposes of a dynastic politics that is substantially of a mediaeval character; but in respect of the measure of success which this anachronistic enterprise meets with, these European powers, while differing greatly among themselves, each and several fall short of the Japanese pattern by a long interval.[1]

But Veblen did not think such a combination would last. In the long run the industrial system must ruin the mental and institutional structure of old Japan. The existing rulers would have their chance of conquest—and would probably seize it—during the intervening period.

The opportunity of Imperial Japan as a fearsome power in the world's concert of dynastic politics may by consequence confidently be expected to lie within the historical interval that so intervenes between Japan's acquirement of the western state of the industrial arts and its consequent, slower but inevitable, falling into line with those materialistic, commercial, and spendthrift conceptions of right and honest living that make the outcome among the (Christian) peoples that have gone before along the road of industrial dominion and individual self-help.[2]

Veblen did not attribute to Imperial Germany the 'responsibility' for the First World War in the same sense as the Allies' propaganda had done.[3] In Veblen's opinion there was after all only a difference of degree between the foreign policy of Germany and that of the other European powers. 'Had there been no Imperial Germany included in the concert of nations, the outcome might not have been substantially different in the long run, so far as regards Europe's eventual fortunes in respect of peace and war; but with Germany included there has been no room to doubt that, whenever this prospective war should break out,

[1] *Essays in Our Changing Order*, New York, 1934, p. 251.
[2] Ibid., p. 255.
[3] 'There can be no harm in recognizing the entire disingenuousness of all parties to the controversy. That the German volume of prevarication is the larger is something of a fortuitous circumstance, due to their more urgent diplomatic need. With the same opportunities and provocation it is doubtful if British diplomacy would not have done just as well, and it is not doubtful that the Russians would have done better' (Note, p. 258, *Imperial Germany and the Industrial Revolution*, New York, 1915).

Germany would be the seat of the disturbance, whether on the offensive or defensive.'[1]

Veblen and Schumpeter, putting aside the interminable quarrel about responsibility, justly remarked that the militaristic spirit surviving from the past dominated the 'dynastic state' of Imperial Germany more than the state in England, where absolutism had been defeated centuries before, or the French Republic born of popular revolution. But they did not claim that this imperialist survival was the only cause of the outbreak or that the rivalry between sovereign states, even non-imperialist ones, would be essentially peaceful. Of all the European states, Germany was the only one capable of conceiving an ambition to dominate, the only one that could, if victorious, impose its rule over the whole of the old continent. She behaved as the other dominant nations of the continent had done before her.

Would she have escaped this imperial temptation if she had been more purely capitalistic and less feudal, if the *bourgeoisie* of the Rhineland, Bavaria, or Westphalia instead of the junkers of Mecklenbourg or East Prussia had held first place? Let us put the question in terms of the future instead of the past. Would the dominant state in an international system refrain from abusing its power and would it succeed in not arousing envy, if it were entirely civil and if industrialism had obliterated all trace of the *ancien régime*? Is the will to conquest or to power, which Comte thought already anachronistic in his time, likely to be recognized for what it is by the governing classes and by the people, once the old prejudices have disappeared? The desire for collective glory, the pride of participation in national greatness, even as one of the lowest of citizens or servants, may well survive in the age of canons, skyscrapers, and underground stations adorned with marble.

Moreover, neither German imperialism which burst out in 1939, nor Japanese imperialism which culminated in 1941, is, in its latest stages, the expression of a feudal class or of the spirit of the *ancien régime*. Here and there a small part of the old governing class opposed totalitarianism out of respect for liberal or Christian values and repugnance for the relapse into bar-

[1] *Imperial Germany and the Industrial Revolution*, p. 259.

barism. The picture of a simple duality—past against future, imperialism against industrial society—does not represent the complexity of the real situation. Imperialists are no more recruited exclusively from the old classes in modern Europe than they were in ancient Rome. The charismatic leaders of popular factions are driven farther by the delirium of power than are the inheritors of the feudal spirit and of 'defensive militarism'. The militarism of the masses is more violent and more dangerous than that of the traditional nobility.

The war of 1914 was initially the result of a diplomatic failure magnified by alliances into a war of hegemony, rather than the consequence of a German will to conquest. The peoples who had been freed by industrialism and the accidents of political history from the heritage of the *ancien régime* showed scarcely less enthusiasm for war than those who had retained a military caste and respect for aristocratic values. The cult of violence and the lust for power became most intense at a time when, as a result of wars and revolutions, a popular élite had finally suppressed the old aristocracy.

The other theory which enables us to ignore the lessons of the twentieth century and to maintain a belief in the pacific nature of industrial civilization is that of Marx, or rather of the Marxists, according to whom wars are the inevitable outcome of the contradictions of capitalism. According to them, the concept of industrial society is misleading since it includes two fundamentally different régimes, capitalism and socialism. The first is essentially bellicose, the second pacific. Comte was not mistaken, and Marx basically agrees with him, in opposing two alternatives: man's struggle with nature and the struggle of men with each other. When the former has ended in victory, the latter will abate of its own accord. Once men are able to exploit the forces of nature, they will no longer wish to fight and kill or enslave each other. In fact, industrialism is essentially incompatible with militarism. But the essence of industrial society will not be revealed until classes and the class war have been overcome and the exploitation of man by man has been eliminated.

In the writings of Marx the theory is not without ambiguity.

Is it the control over nature, i.e. scientific and technological progress, which is decisive, or is it the elimination of classes which is to bring about social and international peace? If the coming of socialism depended upon the development of productive forces this question would not be important. Socialism—the triumph of the proletariat—could not precede economic and social maturity, i.e. the establishment, in the heart of the old society, of the relations of production of the society of the future. But this exact correspondence which is another form of the belief in providence (men only set themselves problems which they can solve) has not been maintained. Consequently, the question inevitably arises: is one type of industrial society as such bellicose and the other pacific?

The necessary relation between capitalism and war has usually been demonstrated in two stages: capitalism implies imperialist expansion, and this in turn culminates inevitably in war between empires. An enormous literature has been devoted to this theory. To what extent, and in what sense, is a régime based on private ownership of the instruments of production and the mechanisms of the market constrained to territorial expansion? In order to show the necessity of territorial expansion the economist must prove, in a formal analysis, that such an economy cannot function as a closed system, that it cannot procure either the raw materials or the outlets that it needs. The first hypothesis—the need for raw materials—calls for a factual verification or refutation, and in any case it does not connect expansion with the régime but with the lack of resources of a country whatever the form of government. The second hypothesis is that of a market economy which would be essentially incapable of absorbing its products, and which would therefore be obliged to have resort to non-capitalist countries for dumping surplus producer goods or consumer goods which purchasing power within the capitalist zone was inadequate to absorb.

Such a demonstration, which was attempted by Rosa Luxembourg, always takes the form of positing a certain rate of surplus value and of accumulation of surplus value in the two sectors (production goods and consumption goods) and of concluding that, at a certain stage in the economic cycle, a disharmony will emerge between the structure of production and the distribution of purchasing power. If this is so, one may infer that the rate of accumulation is not the same in the two sectors, or that the relative importance of the sectors should continually change. The model does not even allow us to conclude that these re-adjustments necessarily take place through economic crises.[1]

On the other hand, it is very easy to explain, in historical terms, the tendency to territorial expansion of a system based upon private property and a market economy. The entrepreneur, whose specific aim is profit, tries to sell at the highest price and to buy at the lowest. The under-developed countries have often provided an opportunity for especially high profits. European industries found in them both raw materials and outlets for manufactured products. It cannot be demonstrated that the English economy in the nineteenth century could not have functioned if it had not sold its cotton goods in India. But it is a fact that, in the primary period of industrialization, it is convenient to have dependable outlets for commodities which the low wages necessitated by a high rate of investment would have difficulty in absorbing.

If territorial expansion was, though not theoretically inevitable, historically connected with the capitalist system, how far can it be regarded as a source of conflict between different economies? So far as expansion results in conditions which approach the ideal market, the capitalist countries would theoretically have no motives for conflict. But in fact, expansion has usually been preceded, accompanied, or followed by the assumption of political sovereignty. This produces more or less substantial advantages for the metropolis and disadvantages for the countries which are excluded. In this sense, colonial empires are a cause of conflicts since different powers use political means to retain, in the territories under their control, privileges in the supply of raw materials or in access to markets.

Colonial conquests are not the only causes of conflict brought about by economic competition between nations. Schumpeter, in his study of imperialism, not only emphasized the survivals of feudalism in Imperial Germany, but pointed out the role of trusts

---

[1] The need to include non-capitalist countries in the economic process does not imply the establishment of political sovereignty over them.

and showed how heavy industry monopolized the internal market, sold its products there above the market price, and had to sell abroad at dumping prices to increase output to the maximum. Such practices, which violate the rules of honest competition, are as inimical as colonial conquest to harmonious and peaceful relations between capitalist countries.

Economic expansion (the search for raw materials, high rates of profit, and markets) and the attempt to obtain, by economic or political means, illegitimate advantages over competitors, are phenomena which undoubtedly existed during the centuries of capitalist development. But the Marxist theory of imperialism goes far beyond these incontestable facts. It claims to relate imperialism to a definite stage of capitalism (monopoly capitalism) and to connect European wars with the struggle to share out the world. Now these relationships, whether they are expressed in terms of historical trends or cause–effect relations, are extremely dubious.

Europe's colonial conquests occupy a period from the sixteenth to the twentieth century. European imperialism could not have been wholly the expression of monopoly capitalism,[1] since it largely preceded it. The domination of finance capitalism (a term borrowed from Hilferding) was much less general than Lenin asserted. Neither the banks nor the international combines divided the world between them, and they were not committed to unleashing a general war if they failed to agree upon the division. Historical study does not reveal the alleged interdependence between the various series of events.

Europe was the world's banker in the nineteenth century, especially in the second half of the century. France had about 40 milliards of gold francs invested abroad on the eve of the First World War, and Great Britain $2\frac{1}{4}$ times as much. In the decade before 1914 the latter country invested abroad every year 5–6 per cent. of its national income. Undoubtedly, these capital movements, whose extent seems to us half a century later almost incredible, were connected with a certain distribution of income within the

---

[1] This concept moreover seems to me itself unacceptable. Capitalism at the end of the nineteenth century and the beginning of the twentieth was neither defined nor dominated by the 'monopolies'.

country. The monetary stability which lasted for a century favoured the possessors of capital and tended to increase inequality. But this diffusion of European capital was on the whole neither the cause nor the effect of colonial conquests, since for the most part French, English, and German capital was placed outside the territories under the sovereignty of these three countries. The greater part of French capital was used as an instrument of diplomacy, English capital was looking for high rates of profit, and German capital was serving the interests of foreign trade as well as of the lenders. Colonial conquest was not necessary to clear the way for investments at high interest rates, and it was rarely the consequence of such investments or a measure taken to protect them.

It is true that at the end of the nineteenth century the countries of Europe plunged into the scramble for Africa and that this continent was divided between the capitalist powers, Asia being no longer available and America being closed to European enterprise by the decision of the U.S.A. One cannot dogmatically deny all connexion between the development of capitalism in Europe and the expansion of colonial empires in Africa. But there is even greater difficulty in discerning a necessary relation. France had neither surplus population nor an industry in need of markets; she had surplus capital but hardly invested it at all in her empire. Germany, in spite of her high birth-rate and economic growth, was the last to become interested in colonies. The civil servants of the Wilhelmstrasse were much more excited than were the bankers or industrialists about Morocco. In each particular case of colonial conquest, one could discover sectional interests, of a firm, or a bank, or a large company, and one may visualize the representatives of these interests laying siege to ministers and extracting their support. But considered as a whole the conquest of Africa by the European nations seems as much the counterpart of continental peace as the effect of a desire for economic exploitation. In the case of France, officers, explorers, adventurers, and missionaries cleared the way and found a career open to their ambition; the ministers and diplomats followed. When one country had secured the sovereignty of a certain African territory, the unwritten law of European rivalry implied that the other countries should obtain compensation. Thus the division of Africa was the by-product of diplomatic practices and of the European balance of power. France had a large share, not because she needed it economically, but because Germany, saturated on the continent, was delighted that the attention of the French should be turned away from the blue line of the Vosges.

Colonial imperialism is still less the cause of European war. Lenin dogmatically asserts that wars are waged on the continent, but the stakes are overseas possessions. He offers no argument to support this assertion. Now, it can be established that:

1. The capitalist countries were not driven to the war by internal contradictions or by the need for expansion.
2. All the diplomatic crises which had colonial conflicts as their cause or their background were resolved peacefully.
3. The war broke out when a conflict in the Balkans aroused national passions and upset the European balance of power. The nations of the Old Continent which dominated the world had every interest in avoiding a struggle to the death. When Comte spoke of the Western Republic and when Renan evoked the amity of Germany, England, and France, they were not predicting the actual course of history but they expressed historical reason. If useless or catastrophic events never occurred, the war of 1914 would not have taken place.

Could it at least be argued that a socialist industrial civilization, without either private ownership of the instruments of production or international competition, would escape such emotional entanglements and would eliminate the economic–political conflicts of imperialism? Since all the relations between economies—foreign trade and capital movements—would be public, the conflicts produced by competition between capitalist concerns or by measures taken against a foreign private company would by definition disappear. But the public character of international economic relations would not eliminate every motive of conflict.

It has been convincingly shown that market prices are not always equitable and that the power which results from the economic importance of each party influences the conditions of exchange. A developed country is in a position to exploit the underdeveloped country when buying food or raw materials, not below the market price but at a freely established price favourable to the industrialized country, which is purchasing primary products whose price is subject to great variations owing to the non-elasticity of demand. The market, it is true, does not guarantee equity, which is moreover difficult to define. But the suppression of a market and the determination of price by agreement between governments gives no greater guarantee. Yugoslavia and Poland have protested against the prices at which the Russians buy their raw materials. After October 1956 the price of Polish coal was raised retrospectively. Yet there remains in this case one relatively objective method of determining the value of commodities: prices in the capitalist market. If this objective measure were eliminated, how arbitrarily prices might be determined by negotiations between socialist countries of unequal power.

It may be objected that conflicts limited to the determination of prices would not arouse popular passions or provoke a serious crisis. If the conditions of exchange between socialist countries alone were in question there would be no ground for resorting to violence. But capitalist countries, in spite of the legends, have not made great wars in order to save their investments, or to buy at the lowest price and to sell at the highest. Great Britain has remained the ally of the U.S.A. which has robbed her of the first place in the world economy. The spread of socialism would only guarantee peace on condition that the domination of weak by strong states was also abolished, and that the rivalry between independent sovereign states was effaced by a new feeling of brotherhood between peoples and nations.

Whatever the social system, industrial society gives rise to many causes of conflict, but never to causes for a struggle to the death, since the common interest in peace is always greater than the limited or marginal interests which oppose it. But no economic system by itself excludes the risk of war, because none ends the state of nature which reigns among rival sovereign states. None guarantees that states will cease to attribute to each other sinister designs, or that they will prefer co-operation to domination and compromise to combat. At the beginning of the century it was not capitalism but international life itself, with its commercialized nationalisms, ideological imperialisms, and the rival wills to power which bore war within itself as the sea bears the tempest.

III

Auguste Comte treated Europe as the centre of the world and the nations of Western Europe as the vanguard of history. The Western Republic which was to reconcile and unite France, England, Germany, and Spain would serve as a model and guide to the rest of humanity. A century later, this Republic is not so far from existing (apart from the exclusion of Spain, whose régime, which is neither liberal nor democratic, is inspired by the *ancien régime*), but it does not occupy the first rank in the competition between states. The U.S.A. is both richer and more powerful, the U.S.S.R. is more powerful.

In spite of this historical decline with regard to the relations between powers, Western Europe illustrates one of the possible methods of pacification as a consequence of industrialism. This pacification does not differ fundamentally from the peace of the positive era as it was conceived by Comte. The nation, conscious of itself, has become a state, frontiers are no longer matters of passionate contention, the different classes of society collaborate, social mobility permits the rise of the most gifted, the inheritance of occupations has disappeared, the transmission of privileges from one generation to the next has been, not eliminated (for this is probably neither possible nor desirable in any society) but diminished, or compensated by the chances of promotion offered to many people.

Neither in the Scandinavian democracy nor in the British is there a military caste. Something of the spirit of the *ancien régime* survives in the castles of the British countryside, in the House of Lords, and in the Coronation ceremony, but the aristocratic past no longer dominates everyday politics. As for transcendant religion, it has been so impregnated and transformed by modern ideas that it renders some of the services which Comte expected of the positivist religion. It does not turn men away from the just organization of communal life on earth, and it inculcates a spirit of reform without bestowing upon any party or theory the seal of the absolute. Bringing down the mighty and raising the humble, careful to recall but not to excuse the imperfections in any human order, religion performs a social function without abandoning its dogmas (which Comte thought anachronistic).

The British or Swedish Welfare State and the *soziale Marktwirtschaft* of the German Federal Republic differ in many respects from the positive society of which Comte dreamed. He had little sympathy with parliaments, and even that of Westminster would not perhaps have obtained his unqualified approval. Neither public opinion, nor intellectuals, nor churches, provide the equivalent of the spiritual power which was to regulate feelings and bring men together. Without doubt, the founder of positivism would have considered that in Western democracies the desire for gain overcomes devotion to the community. The acquisitive society has not yet been controlled and regulated by an altruistic morality.

In spite of these reservations, the example of Germany[1] is the most striking example of historical change from militarism to industrialism. The old military class having been eliminated, the vanquished seem to have become more peace-loving than their conquerors. Protests against rearmament increase in Germany (and in Japan), as if the nations which had suffered most from the evil had been most completely cured of it. The country which was the cradle of imperialism in Europe has plunged into peaceful industrialism with an ardour equal to that which formerly inspired its soldiers.

The pacification of Western Europe is still of too short duration to permit any general conclusions to be based upon it. Above all, it is too easily explained by circumstances for us to dare to see in it the beginning of a new era. After the collapse of the dreams of empire, men turned to other work, desires, and ambitions. The pacification of the Western Republic might be the result of defeat and the expression of historical resignation. The peace which reigns within and between the nations of Western Europe may

[1] And also of Japan. The parallel between Germany and Japan has continued since the Second World War.

well be, in the post-Second World War situation, an exception to the spirit of the time, rather than its symbol.

Since 1945 there has probably been no year without war, and even apart from war in the legal meaning of the term (conflict between internationally recognized states), violence has been rampant, revolutions have multiplied, and men have been massacred in hundreds of thousands, sometimes in millions.[1]

In Asia, Indonesia and Indo-China have attained their independence by a war against the colonial power. The countries which achieved independence without war (Burma, India, Pakistan) have experienced civil war (Burma is still in its throes) or a half war between the successor states (the question of Kashmir is still not settled). After the civil war had ended in China, Korea became the scene of a conflict between the two pseudo-states of the North and South, encouraged and extended by the rivalry between the Soviet Union and China on the one hand and the U.S.A. on the other. The troubles have now reached the Near East and Africa (Kenya and Algeria). The revolt of the Mau-Mau has not initiated a war according to the meaning of the word in international law any more than has the Algerian rebellion. On the day when the Algerian rebels form a 'free government' in Cairo or Tunisia and when this government is recognized by some foreign states, the Algerian guerilla army will assume a different legal form without changing its nature.

If the pacification of Western Europe does not justify optimism about the future, neither does the violence raging in the under-developed countries justify pessimism, if one refers to the categories of Comte. Those regions of the world which are not at peace are backward in relation to modern civilization. As yet, neither the formation of nation-states nor industrialism has overcome the conflicts of the past. Religion divides rather than unites groups, sects are arrayed against each other, and rival minorities claim to represent nations which would require decades or centuries to create and which the impatience of the masses and the weariness of the European powers call forth from one day to the next.

[1] Millions were massacred after the declaration of independence of India and Pakistan.

After all, Comte did not state the precise route which non-Western man would follow in order to join its *avant-garde*, any more than Karl Marx speculated on the different ways in which the nations would ·achieve socialism. Violence in Asia, the Near East, and Africa, is born of the contradictions between the traditional régimes and Western influences. It is comparable with that which raged in Europe in previous centuries. The Japanese attempt at conquest was in part an imitation of the example given by the Europeans who profited from their industrial progress to colonize other nations. The existence of violence which results from the development of industrialism and whose end is the constitution of nations, does not refute the positivist theory of the peaceful vocation of modern civilization.

Where should we seek the confirmation or refutation of Comte's theses? It would seem that only the behaviour of those nations which are most advanced on the road of industrialism and which have not been reduced to passivity by recent defeats, can provide an answer.

It is, however, an ambiguous answer, since the antagonism of the two giants suggests that industrial civilization offers no fewer occasions for ideological warfare than past civilizations, and also that the apparently fundamental hostility does not inevitably degenerate, in our era, into war to the death. The pessimist will emphasize the irreducible hostility, and the optimist the strange alliance against war which seems to unite the U.S.A. and the Soviet Union, in spite of their many obvious disagreements. Is it industrialism which halts the two Great Powers on the road to war? Is it industrialism which creates between them an insuperable antagonism?

In the geometry of diplomatic relations, the present situation so far as Europe and America are concerned does not present any very original features. Two states peripheral to Western Europe, the cradle of industrial civilization, have, because of their size and because of the European wars, come to dominate the scene. Any bi-polar structure is by itself unstable. A shared hegemony is a contested hegemony. The same diplomatic geometry which accounts for the cold war also explains the temporary absence of violence. Neither of the two Great Powers is in mortal peril.

Neither sees its vital interests threatened. Only the passion to rule could draw them into a death struggle. Two-thirds of humanity remain outside the European-American system; and the nation which gained control of this system would not at once become master of the masses of Asia or Africa.

If one thinks in military terms, the winner of a third world war would apparently have attained universal domination. He would not encounter any rival worthy of him. But appearances are deceptive here. It is idle to recall that modern methods of administration and domination are so superior to those of the Roman or Chinese Empires that a universal empire in the conditions of the twentieth century would not be larger than that of the Antonines or the Mings. There is a major difference resulting from industrialism. The societies of the past were economically stagnant. Of course they experienced at certain times periods of economic progress, but the increase of the means of production and the raising of living standards were not a constant aim nor an essential characteristic of their civilization. The emperor who, thanks to his absolute power and an authoritarian bureaucracy, maintained order and permitted the peasant masses to live, had done his duty. He unscrupulously exploited his own subjects and those of other races which he had enslaved. There is nothing like this in our own time.

Industry provides the means for destroying masses of people, as Hitler's example has shown. If the fancy took him, the conqueror could exterminate whole nations, millions, tens of millions of human beings. But the principal ambition of conquerors is not to exterminate but to enslave. And enslavement in our time no longer pays.[1] For work to pay dividends it must be skilled, and for it to be skilled the worker must have had a minimum of education. But slaves cannot be taught without acquiring a desire to escape from their slavery. Hitler carried to an extreme the conqueror's anachronistic madness in the century of industrial civilization; to exterminate evil races, to treat what were held to be inferior peoples as subhuman and to confine them to the servile occupations. Imperialism had to degenerate into racialism and to fall below the level of ancient or Asiatic imperialisms, in

[1] At least in the majority of cases.

order to have any meaning in a century in which industrialism invites all the nations to work together and offers them the distant prospect of equality.

The Soviet Union has continued, in Eastern Europe, the imperialism of Hitler and has imposed a system which is perhaps in some ways as detestable as that of the Third Reich. But there is a difference; the Soviet Union keeps abreast of the times. Her ideology, if not her institutions, is that characteristic of industrial civilization. For this very reason she cannot escape the contradictions inherent in imperialism in the age of democracy and machine production.

After the victory of 1945 the Soviet armies did not reject the traditional benefits of conquest; they subjected the vanquished to the pleasure of the soldiery, they pillaged, dismantled machinery, and appropriated the products of the factories. Industrialism does not exclude these traditional processes of enrichment. But what are these levies compared with the volume of goods which each year result from collective work? If one wants to prolong the pillage one must appropriate without payment, or at very low prices, the raw materials, producer goods, and manufactured goods of the conquered people. The Soviet rulers, imprisoned in an ideology in which they believe after a fashion, aimed, in instituting régimes modelled on that of Imperial Russia, to promote what they call socialism, and in any case, to establish a heavy industry and to develop natural and human resources. In the long run, the combination of these two undertakings—exploitation by the parent state and a high rate of investment—results in an intolerable reduction of the standard of living in the satellite states. Since 1956 the Soviet Union has been obliged to aid those countries which she has colonized. That domination is costly instead of being profitable is a new fact and derives from the conditions of industrial society. It cannot but influence international relations.

Analogous phenomena, only even more pronounced, have appeared in the Western world. The hegemony exercised by the U.S.A. was at once reflected in unprecedented budgets for foreign aid. Since the end of the Second World War, the European nations have expended in their colonies, empires, or overseas possessions, however one chooses to call them, as much or more than they have received from their American protector. France, apart from the war in Indo-China and Algeria, has spent every year in the French Union 200–300 milliard francs at 1955 prices, or 700–900 million dollars. When political domination involves the obligation to promote social development, and thus to raise the standard of living of the population, it ceases to enrich the metropolitan power. In this century the glory of governing has to be its own reward.

The two giants proclaim the right of peoples to self-determination and the duty of rich nations to help poor ones. Ideological considerations do not prevent the Soviet Union from refusing to Hungary the right of secession any more than they have prevented her from exploiting the People's Democracies. States have never been absolutely faithful to the ideas by which they claim to be directed, but nor are they ever entirely uninfluenced by them. Legally and formally the states of Eastern Europe are independent, and legal forms are not without real consequences in the long run. The Soviet rulers are driven to reduce their levies on the satellite economies so as not to weaken the so-called socialist régimes they have established, because these régimes need an ideology and the practice of exploitation ends by discrediting the ideology. Similarly, the U.S.A. can here and there buy raw materials at a price lower than the underdeveloped countries or an impartial observer would deem equitable. But a universal empire would none the less impose on the U.S.A., even if they were not threatened by the Soviet Union and were the sole rulers of the planet, more obligations than economic advantages.

In still another way industrialism tends to divert the Great Powers from a fight to the death. Comte saw the proof that pacifism was peculiar to industrial society in the mediocrity of the 'destructive machines' available to states. He was right about the French armies of his time which, since the Restoration, had made no progress beyond the armies of the Empire and indeed tended to regress as a result of the traditionalism of the general staffs. Since that time, war has stimulated the engineers and military leaders. The nations have fully exploited scientific and technical resources in the development of 'destructive machines'. The present situation is thus the opposite of that which Comte observed. The technical stagnation of the armies seemed to him proof of the pacifism of industrial societies. Atomic and hydrogen bombs, stratospheric bombers and rockets demonstrate the excessive interest which the nations take in the engines of war. But once these weapons are available, they may perhaps reduce the risk of an outbreak by the fear which they inspire. Even if the fruits of victory were world hegemony—and what kind of hegemony would there be over ruined towns, vast provinces contaminated by radioactive dust, and men scattered in search of an impossible protection—the dangers and the cost would be sufficient to dissuade any leader who retained his common sense, or thought in economic terms, from such an adventure. Nobody is insane enough to let loose voluntarily a thermo-nuclear war.[1]

Is industrial society responsible for the antagonism itself, which it contains within certain limits? The two ideologies, Soviet and Western, both originated in industrial society. They have many points in common: the secularization of aspirations, the cult of technology, the organization of the masses, indefinitely increasing production, and the transformation of the future. The conflict of the two ideologies reproduces the nineteenth-century conflict between liberal optimism and the catastrophic optimism of the Marxists. But in spite of appearances, the two schools have drawn closer together because the so-called revolutionary ideology, embodied in imperfect régimes, has lost the prestige of the unknown, the transcendant, that which has never been seen.

As the object of faith becomes increasingly immanent and beliefs are more and more concerned with the organization of the collectivity, political ideologies clash in the industrial period as did religions in the theological epoch. Comte only imagined an ideological war between the survivors of the *ancien régime* and the supporters of the progressive spirit. But the latter is no more unified than was the theological or metaphysical spirit. Societies dispute about the definition of the good society as much as about the notion of the true God.

---

[1] Unless he could be certain of destroying the enemy's means of retaliation, i.e. of striking the other dead and of being spared himself.

Thus the bellicose peace between the two Great Powers, while not lacking precedents, none the less presents some original features. The U.S.A. and the Soviet Union are both masters of half the economically developed world; they are rivals who cannot agree officially on the division of the European-American region, but who prefer not to engage in a struggle to the death. The course of a war is unpredictable, but whatever the outcome the ruins would be piled monstrously under an empty sky. Neither of these states needs a universal empire, nor is the existence of either of them threatened. Industrialism contributes both to the impossibility of agreement and to the refusal to make the supreme test. The new powers of destruction make the bravest hearts tremble, the responsibility for economic growth reduces the attraction of conquest, and the ideology of each Great Power for the time being prohibits reconciliation.

At the end of the first half of the century those pessimists who predicted a conflagration into which rich and powerful European societies would insanely plunge their youth and their wealth seemed to be justified by events; neither industry nor the *bourgeoisie* had prevented European nations from following in the path of the Greek cities and ruining each other in warfare. Twelve years after the end of the Second World War, twelve years after the destruction of Hiroshima and Nagasaki, hope revives, or at least a doubt emerges. After all, may there not be some truth in Comte's optimism?

It is not that we are living in a time of peace. As we have seen, the underdeveloped countries are ravaged by armed strife and the machine-gun has more influence there than the ballot paper. But the underdeveloped countries live on the threshold of industrial civilization. The nations of Europe, in spite of their diminished power and the loss of their empires, enjoy a standard of living higher than at any time in their glorious past. They have discovered the vanity of conquest, and within nations all social classes share in the hardships and the profits of labour. What is the use of violence when the future may satisfy the dreams of the unprivileged without involving the ruin of those who are considered today as privileged?

As for the two giants, a conflict of principles arrays one against the other, but the community of industrial civilization restrains them from crossing the line which separates a bellicose peace from a fight to the death, limited war from total war. The winner of a third world war would hold sway over ruins, and probably the only victor would be the country, if there were such a one, which had remained on the fringe of the battlefield. Or, in other words, there would be no victor, only survivors. With Europe and America devastated by thermo-nuclear bombs, China would continue the adventure of mankind.

In the first half of the century wars were typical of industrial civilization, but of an initial phase of this civilization. The excess of production in relation to the basic needs of the population made available for warfare immense resources of men and materials. All the belligerents proceeded to total mobilization, and workers in field and factory made a contribution no less indispensable than soldiers at the front. Throwing in the whole of their forces, the conflicting sides sought total victory, not in the sense of destroying the enemy state but in the more limited meaning of enforcing its capitulation. The armistice of 1918 left the German empire at the mercy of the allies. The unconditional capitulation of 1945 temporarily suspended the existence of the German state and, to some extent, of Japanese sovereignty.

In spite of this total mobilization and victory, the industrial wars of the twentieth century resembled those of the past. In certain respects they were even less destructive, for destruction is measured not absolutely but relatively, and the capacity for recuperation, human and material, had increased more than the power of destructive machines. After the Thirty Years War the German population had diminished by half. The war of 1914 cost the equivalent of the additional population which would have resulted from ten years of peace. The French and the German populations were larger in 1950 than in 1939. Ten years after the end of the war the German towns are rebuilt and production and living standards are higher than before the catastrophe.

The consequences of wars cannot be measured only in figures. It is true, as is often said, that Europe has lost its world leadership on the battlefields of the Marne and Flanders, and in the plains of Poland and Russia, and that it has received injuries there of which the disintegration of overseas empires is the inevitable consequence. In a more subtle and profound way, the fascist and communist despotic régimes, which before 1914 would have seemed contrary to historical evolution, have reflected the monstrous growth in the power of the state with the mobilization of materials, men, and knowledge that total war required.

The total war of the recent past, more destructive spiritually than materially, reflected the technology of coal, steel, and the railway, and later of the internal combustion engine and aviation. The energy came from the soil (oil, petrol) and explosives were of a chemical kind. The destructive machines were relatively simple. Wars were already economically irrational, so far as the mass of the population was concerned, but the latter's views might be mistaken. The identification of territorial conquests with trade outlets and of extension of sovereignty with increase of wealth, though not rationally justified, was not absurd. The hesitations of judgement between the cost of a war and the benefits of domination which would have made the Germans the master race, were psychologically intelligible. After all, ordinary citizens seem to find joy and pride in the victories of their sportsmen; why should they be indifferent to military victories?

From 1945 we enter upon a different technological era. A war conducted at the level of modern technology would use explosives fired by atomic energy, and electronic and ballistic weapons. This means a reversal of the relationship between destructive power and capacity to recover. The damage caused by a thermonuclear war fought to the finish could not be repaired in a few years. In the First World War the industrial organization of the factories was practically undamaged and continued to supply the colossal war machine to the very end. During the Second World War, in spite of bombing, war production in Germany increased up to 1945. The destruction of residential areas did not prevent the continuation of work in the factories. It needed the proximity of the air bases and daytime precision bombing to paralyse Germany's industrial machine in the spring of 1945, by the destruction of transport and certain carefully selected factories.

All that we know of the power of the atomic and hydrogen

bombs indicates that the fabric of industrial civilization would not stand up to attacks with thermo-nuclear weapons. It would no longer be a question of progressive mobilization or of maintaining fighting strength by the work of millions of men. If the unimaginable horror of such a total war (i.e. waged with all available weapons) were to come about in spite of everything, no one can predict what would happen after the initial stage (a few days or hours). Everyone knows that industrial civilization would be threatened with annihilation by its inordinate destructive power.

The present situation is almost the exact opposite of that envisaged by Comte. He saw the proof of the fundamental pacifism of modern societies in the mediocrity of their 'destructive machines', so inferior to what science could invent and manufacture. Today a conflict of principle and power arrays the two giants against each other. The populations of Africa and Asia feel an obviously strong resentment against the white minority which was dominant yesterday and is today still privileged. We are not deceived by the hope of a rapid pacification. The peace required by the logic of industrial civilization, peace within a universal system of belief, or based upon mutual respect for each other's beliefs, and upon the exploitation in common of natural resources for the benefit of all, is at present ruled out by passions and by ideologies. Between the absurdity of total war and the impossibility of real peace, the hopes of humanity are confined to the possibility of limiting warfare.

The industrial civilization of coal and steel allowed of the mobilization of soldiers, tanks, and aeroplanes. Industrial civilization in the electronic and atomic era can only escape suicide by the limitation of warfare—limiting the number of belligerents, the area of operations, resources used, and objectives pursued—but there is one limitation which conditions all the others. If neither side is to push the use of force to an extreme, it is necessary that neither should feel in danger of extinction, that neither should want to extort unconditional surrender from the other, and that neither should attempt to attain objectives incompatible with the vital interests of the other. In short, limited war implies the resolve of the Great Powers to tolerate each other.

Industrial civilization whose cities, weapons, and rockets are all characterized by lack of restraint can only escape the apocalypse by moderation.

Thus we have arrived at the anxieties of the present day. Can we legitimately forget them and, like the philosophers of last century, speculate about what the future may bring? I am aware of the audacity of this attempt, which is contrary to the positivist approach, not as Comte conceived it but as it is understood by contemporary sociologists. To diminish my responsibility, I shall disclaim in advance any pretension to foresee the future. I do not know whether the industrial civilization of the atom and of electronics will accomplish that limitation of war which the industrial civilization of coal and steel could not achieve. I shall merely make a *mental experiment*: in what conditions is it possible to conceive the transition from non-total war, founded on mutual fear, to a peace based upon the desire for non-violence?

The principal conditions appear to me to be three in number: a diminution of the gulf between the privileged minority and the mass of humanity which remains sunk in poverty; the constitution of nations ready to accept each other within an international community; and the end of the conflict between the two Great Powers and the two dominant ideologies, which implies that the various countries concerned would be ready to recognize the kinship between the different types of industrial civilization.

The first condition—diminution of the gap between the standard of living of the Western minority on the one hand and the African and Asiatic masses on the other—does not in theory seem unrealizable. In this connexion it would be a mistake to return to the classical controversy of last century between optimists and pessimists. That controversy concerned historical predictions, not theoretical problems.

We can now specify exactly the circumstances in which industrialism actually improves the lot of the greatest number, and on the other hand, the circumstances in which it creates little islands of modernity while increasing the misery of those who do not escape from the traditional institutions. In abstract terms, one may say that it is necessary and sufficient that the rate of economic development should surpass that of demographic growth.

No system, whether of private or public ownership, whether it has a market or a planned economy, can escape this fundamental requirement. The product per head of population never ceased to grow in Japan between the beginning of the Meiji era and 1930, in spite of the rapid increase in population. The product per head in India has probably been increasing for the past few years although there is no assurance that the sub-continent has definitely emerged from the vicious circle of poverty.

International organizations have calculated the number of millions of dollars of investments necessary, given a certain rate of demographic growth, for the product per head (or the standard of living) to rise by a certain percentage. I do not attach any great significance to this kind of statistics. No one knows exactly what is the average rate of return on capital for the whole of the so-called underdeveloped countries. A solution would not be miraculously achieved by converting present military expenditure to economic aid. In order to break the vicious circle of poverty, it is not sufficient to put millions of dollars at the disposal of millions of men. The latter must also be in a position to spend the millions on sound investments, and this requires that machines be available in developed countries and the programmes, workshops, and technicians ready in the underdeveloped countries. Economic aid can certainly reduce the sufferings of primary industrialization and make good for a few years the deficit in the balance of trade in a country such as India. But to build an industrial civilization nations must change their ways of life and thought and adopt legal and political institutions often incompatible with their centuries old customs. A colonial power may impose this revolution from without, as the Soviet Union has done in central Asia, or as France had briefly the inclination to do in Africa. But once colonialism has been eliminated the essential task can only be carried out by the governments of nations which have achieved their independence.

In the short run the prospects are far from favourable. *Decolonization* in certain regions of the world involves a return of capital and technicians to Europe and a lowering of the quality of the administration. Nations emerge which have not reached the level of industrial civilization, and which are the more jealous of their independence the less they have of material means to assure it, and more suspicious of their ex-rulers the more they need them.

At the same time the increase of population continues, sometimes at an accelerated rate, so greatly does medical progress outpace economic development and so much greater are the returns on investments in hygiene than on those in industry. Probably, the number of men who are trapped in the vicious circle of poverty is greater than the number who have entered on the cumulative process of growth.

But the peoples living in poverty are no longer condemned to passivity. One might have thought that in the industrial age when wealth and power are based on technology, the nations enjoying prosperity would easily escape the attacks of nations drawn to adventure and dreams of greatness by hunger and austerity. But this is by no means the case. The Soviet Union has strikingly shown that the greater part of the increase in production, after the satisfaction of basic needs, can be used for the construction of heavy industry and the maintenance of military forces rather than for improving the condition of the masses in proportion to the increase of total resources. The same method can be used by China and other Asian countries. Unable to compete with those in the van, the bulk of humanity can embark upon the pursuit of power which industrial civilization offers as an alternative to the pursuit of abundance.

Even if the wealthy nations are protected from invasion by the weapons of mass destruction, they are not protected from guerilla warfare. In our time, the war of partisans has changed the map of the world more than the classical or atomic destructive machines. A resolute minority can make life unbearable for a ruling class as soon as the masses are more or less sympathetic to it. The cost of fighting against terrorism and partisans soon becomes prohibitive for democratic industrial countries. Constantly menaced by inflation, the latter would need to impose unpopular measures in order to finance repression. The doubts of those groups in which economic calculation is habitual are added to the ideological preferences of the anti-colonialists. Partisan warfare has given the *coup de grâce* to European overseas empires. Will it cease once anti-colonialism has triumphed? Will the governments of liberated nations end a reign of terror which they began in order to get rid of the conquerors? It is to be feared that the return or the achievement of the rule of law is not yet at hand for a part of the human race.

Besides these difficulties we should not forget the significance of the first condition we have formulated. The cumulative process of growth cannot continue indefinitely for any nation (at least in the present state of technology) owing to lack of land. As long as food is not manufactured industrially from raw materials in un-limited supply, and men have to rely upon wheat, rice, meat, or fish that nature produces and reproduces slowly, we cannot imagine societies becoming wealthier, or being able to assure permanently to all their members the standard of living of the present-day American middle class, unless we assume a stationary population. In the short run, the increase of population in the privileged Western minority is not incompatible with either a higher standard of living or the pacification of international relations (it may even be favourable to these two desirable results). It is in the underdeveloped countries that the main-tenance of the traditional birth-rate, with modern or semi-modern conditions of hygiene, prevents the increase in productive capa-city from leading to an improvement in the conditions of the masses. Confident in their Western experience, many observers believe that economic progress will have the same consequences in Asia, Africa, and South America as it had in Europe and that it will result in such a decline in the birth-rate that the standard of all will rise as everyone's labour becomes more productive.

Even if we accept this optimistic view (and in any case it can-not be verified for decades) a halt in the demographic growth of the whole of humanity must be made some day or other if we are to prevent the disproportion between needs and resources from inciting individuals and communities to seek their own salvation at the expense of others.

However far off it may be, this first condition does not seem *essentially* unrealizable. In the U.S.A. one can see approximately what the stationary situation would be; in other words, the volume of goods that could be assured and the hours of work that would be necessary in order to provide for the fundamental needs (food, housing, clothing, education), and the division of labour between the various occupations which results from the unequal productivity of industrial, agricultural, and (in the broad sense) administrative work. A stationary population is not unlikely in a society which has attained such a stationary economic state.

On the other hand, the second condition we formulated, the constitution of a world community of nations which mutually accept each other, is ambiguous. It suggests an idea rather than a complex of institutions. The pacification of Western Europe provides a possible model: with their roots in history, the nations wish to retain their identity without regarding each other as enemies. But one may ask whether the renunciation of power politics on the part of the European nations is not an expression of their weakness and of their subordination to the really dominant states. In other words, can one imagine the world completely pacified by the extension and reinforcement of national communities satisfied with their lot and not envious of others?

Probably such a peace, which would be neither imposed from above nor a result of the balance of power, nor due to fear, would require a lowering of barriers between nations, demilitarization, and the transfer of some state powers to a supra-national organization. If we suppose the first condition realized, purely economic conflicts would disappear, the supply of raw materials to each community would no longer be endangered, and natural resources would be exploited in common. The 'commercialized nationalism' of which Thorstein Veblen spoke would disappear, as did the nationalism of dynastic states and of the feudal tradition before it. From that stage different types of organization are conceivable and they all point in the same direction; nations no longer dream of making war and, the economy being less and less confined within national boundaries, national sovereignties tend to fade away or to become administrative units which the citizens are more willing to accept the nearer they are to them. Community of culture and historic unity dedicated to power politics are no longer identical. Sovereign states no longer use industry as their tool and no longer declare that the prosperity of the national industry is their objective. World prosperity being no longer incompatible with the prosperity of individual nations, or rather, the prosperity of all being regarded as necessary to the prosperity of each, communities admit the essentially international (or if you prefer non-national) character of the economic order.

This recognition involves in its turn the fulfilment of the third condition—the disappearance of the conflict of ideologies and of power between today's two giants (or any other giants of the future). The U.S.A. and the Soviet Union, the West and China no longer judge each other's ideals as deceptive and their institutions as criminal. They no longer suspect each other of desiring the death of his rival: they understand the kinship of their dreams and the interdependence of their destiny.

How, it may be objected, will such a reconciliation be possible? Would it not be even more contrary to the facts than the abuse exchanged by the protagonists in this drama? It is not a matter of underestimating the violence or the stakes of contemporary conflict. It would be naïve to expect an early peace. But we should delude ourselves just as much if we thought that the conflict between communism and Western democracy (or between socialism and capitalism) could not be resolved. These two types of industrial society have more characteristics in common than the doctrinaires in the two camps wish to admit and—passions apart—more reasons for coming to an agreement than for destroying each other.

Let us not forget that the Soviets and the West, representing the two types of industrial society, claim to be guided by the same values; both aim to exploit natural resources, to raise the standard of living, and to achieve an economy of abundance. Politically they declare themselves democratic, partisans of the liberation of nations and the rule of the common man. Between Marxists and the West the argument is about the merits of the institutions—property systems, economic methods, political systems—which provide the framework of industrialism. Since the two industrial societies accept the same criteria, it is not impossible to determine their relative value. Economically, a high rate of investment is perhaps desirable for the sake of future generations, but the watchword 'Save, save; this is the law and the prophets' is, according to Marx himself, that of capitalism, not of socialism. That this formula remains indispensable to the East, is proof that the Soviet system is temporarily backward in industrialism, not necessarily permanently inferior to that of the West, which is already capable of distributing to the masses many benefits of technological progress. The Soviets could claim that the higher rate of investment, involving a higher rate of growth and a slower rise in consumption will in time give them an advantage over the West which sacrifices the future to the present. This claim is rather unconvincing because of the low productivity of the collective farms, an increase in food supply being the essential condition for an improvement in the condition of the masses.

Politically, the Soviets are obliged to claim that the single party and the unconditional authority of the general staff of the party is equivalent to the dictatorship of the proletariat (which is absurd). Moreover, this dictatorship itself can only be justified historically; it is only a transitory phase, not the final régime. Is not the citizens' inability to choose their representatives even farther from the democratic ideal than the partial manipulation of free elections? A community which needs the monopoly of a single party thereby shows that it cannot tolerate open controversy and free discussion between individuals or groups. Leaving aside the dictatorship of the party, which is called dictatorship of the proletariat, what will democratization comprise if not the relaxation of ideological orthodoxy or the rise of a multi-party system?

It does not much matter whether or not one agrees with these opinions on the relative value of the two types of industrial society. The essential thing is to admit the kinship between them. If we admit that the ends are the same, the controversy about the advantages of collective or private property, of a planned or a market economy, concerns the means, and is really technical and not metaphysical, even though passion and ideology transform it into a metaphysical, almost a religious quarrel.

The large American corporations differ more from traditional private property, the ownership of a patch of land or a small shop, than from the Soviet trusts. A capitalist régime in which the State is responsible for full employment and the volume of investment, distributes to the masses the surplus production resulting from increasing productivity and allows trade unions the political role of discussing with employers' federations, is more like what was called socialism in the nineteenth century than the image of capitalism which the old-fashioned propagandists of the 'day of judgement' persist in retaining. The economic aspect of the conflict between the Soviet Union and the West calls for compromise and a gradual reconciliation of the two sides of the Iron Curtain rather than war to the death.

The political aspect has quite a different significance. If the West believes that its very existence is threatened, this is not, whatever the doctrinaires of the Soviet system may say, through attachment to free enterprise or to free competition as such. From a technical viewpoint, a certain amount of private property and competition seems to us preferable to the concentration of power, property, and planning which is theoretically for the benefit of the State but in fact for the benefit of the few men who govern the State. But the essential point is that the Soviet régime has brought with it up to now a state ideology and a single-party system; it destroys freedom of thought, individual security, rivalry between parties, and the guarantees of a constitutional authority. Obviously peace does not require that the Soviets should confess their sins and hail the parliamentary democracies as the culmination of human history. But it does at least require that they should no longer claim the single-party system and ideological orthodoxy as the supreme expression of democracy and as a necessary stage on the royal road of humanity.

At the present time the truth or falsity of the Western and Soviet interpretations of the situation has less influence on events than the fact that these interpretations exist, are passionately accepted by millions of people, and are radically opposed. The elements which Comte included in the concept of industrial society are henceforth dissociated. A Soviet régime favours science, industry, and machines, not free inquiry and rational research, which are the essence of industrial society and of the Western spirit. The doctrine which, according to the Soviets, ought to direct the reorganization of society, is not positivism, which preached class co-operation, but Marxism, which declares inevitable the struggle between proletarians and capitalists and sees no hope of peace except in the total victory of the former. Such a doctrine divides humanity, exalts those régimes which accept it, and mercilessly condemns the others; in short, it fosters what Comte called ideological warfare.

The re-establishment of human unity presupposes the universal diffusion or the progressive relaxation of this doctrine. Would the conversion to the Soviet system of the whole of humanity result in peace? If the gap between productive forces and standards of living remained, would the U.S.A. and the Soviet Union, governed by parties paying lip service to Marxism-Leninism, accept their inequality of wealth in an idyllic peace? Until doctrinaire passion, which is today expressed in Marxism-Leninism or Stalinism, has given place to a spirit of scientific inquiry, the interpretation of the ideology officially adopted by the whole of humanity would create almost as many occasions for quarrelling as does the conflict of ideologies in our era. Only the second alternative offers real hope; the Soviet societies, as they progress, should relax the orthodoxy of which they are at present prisoners, and should admit that there are different roads to socialism and that the different stages are characterized less by the nationalization of large enterprises than by the accumulation of capital and the rise in the productivity of labour.

While the differences between standards of living in the West, the Soviet countries, and the underdeveloped countries remain so great, it will be useless to expect the two worlds to accept each other. Anti-Western passions are both expressed and concealed by the doctrine that socialism comes after capitalism in the course of history, whereas the slight development of productive forces and the merciless processes of tyranny in the so-called Socialist countries suggest an inverse relation. In other words, the third condition implies the first. While the differences in resources are immense, the resentment of the underprivileged and the attempt to catch up are inevitable. Ideologies like that of the Soviet Union facilitate effort, camouflage resentment, and substitute ideological progress for economic backwardness. The more the Soviet régimes can give to their citizens the benefits enjoyed by the citizens of capitalist democracies, the less inclined they will be to deny the claims and the real achievements of the latter.

Let it be clearly understood that I do not assert that the equalization of productive capacity or standards of living will suffice to re-establish peace between states and between ideologies. The wars of the twentieth century have been waged between states belonging to the same civilization and having comparable living standards. There is nothing to indicate that the Soviet rulers would renounce their doctrine after the disappearance of the poverty which provides the rational motive we discern in their madness.

If, in our mental experiment, it has seemed possible to realize the three conditions, there are plenty of objections even to such an abstract and hypothetical optimism.

It is true that industrial civilization is favourable to co-operation between classes and nations, that it makes war irrational and peace the interest of all. But it fails to abolish the causes of conflict.

Domination, we have said, no longer pays. The master cannot keep the slave poor indefinitely and he can only raise the living standards of poor nations by costly investments. But there are exceptions to this rule. Great Britain's protectorate in Bahrein and Kuweit is certainly profitable. France's sovereignty in the Sahara would be a source of profit if millions of tons of petroleum lay hidden beneath the burning sands. The ideal colony in the twentieth century is a desert containing black gold. The various emirates of the Arabian peninsular come close to this ideal.

Even if we ignore these marginal cases, any 'politicization' of the economy engenders friction and harms certain interests. If trade between states is planned, will not the strongest impose prices which the weakest will regard as inequitable? If there is free trade, will not the country whose industry loses a market because the goods of a competitor are cheaper, be tempted to defend itself by methods which will set up a chain reaction of resentment and suspicion? While states suspect each other of hostile intentions they are alert to assure, even by force, their supplies of energy and metals. It is even conceivable that wars will (in the long run) be justifiable once more when reserves of raw materials are inadequate to satisfy all needs.[1]

The latter is a very long-term contingency. The other possibilities do not weaken the fundamental proposition that a major war is irrational in the age of industrial civilization, once the whole of humanity has embarked upon the cumulative process of enrichment.

From a political viewpoint, the formation of nations comes up against the obstacle of heterogeneous communities. In Algeria there are a million French people whose average income is at about the same level as that of the French in metropolitan France, and eight million Algerians, three-quarters of whom have an income seven or eight times lower. The dominant French minority would not think of submitting to the laws of an Algerian Republic, and the Mohammedan majority, inspired by nationalism, thinks only of forming an independent state, similar to that of Tunisia or Morocco. In the African continent there are many cases of overlapping communities. Even if the populations of European or Asian extraction agreed to return to their countries of origin (which is inconceivable), any large state would have a heterogeneous population since Africa as a whole has not gone through the process of transition from tribe to nation.

The uncertainty of the results of our mental experiment turns on the third condition. The ideological conflict between the Soviet system and capitalism is not insoluble, because both are aiming at the same objectives and lay claim to the same values. The nature of the conflict is not the same as between the *ancien régime* and the revolution or between the feudal and the industrial spirit. The Soviet system and capitalism are two versions of industrial civilization and, according to the logic of industry, ought to recognize their kinship. But is this logic socially and humanly compelling?

Thus we reach the final uncertainty. Industrial society, as defined by Comte, comprised a way of thinking, a social organi-

[1] Or again, if the cost of exploiting mineral resources available to both parties is so different that it is worth establishing sovereignty over the rich areas with a low cost of production.

zation, and a system of government, and the whole system was incompatible with the spirit of war. Schumpeter and Veblen also considered that the spirit of industrial society was foreign to the prejudices or superstitions which are essential to the survival of the feudal hierarchy, the dynastic state, or aggressive imperialism. Veblen put the blame for war upon what he called 'commercialized nationalism', while the Marxists blamed 'monopoly capitalism'. In the present phase, the survivors of the *ancien régime* use the power of industry to embark upon conquest, with the collusion or at the instigation of commercial or financial interests. Beyond this stage—which is a new formulation of Comte's intermediate stage—the socialists envisaged an economic organization which would prevent rivalry of interests and the methods of power politics. Veblen, after the First World War, suggested a league of peaceful nations which would liquidate both feudal survivals and capitalist speculation.

No one had clearly perceived the major difficulty. The exchanges between politico-economic units are partly distorted by import duties, export subsidies, cartels for maintaining internal prices, dumping, and the search for high rates of profit, which Marxist critics untiringly denounced at the beginning of this century. But if private enterprise and market mechanisms were abandoned, the exchange of goods between economic units with separate sovereignties would become political acts. There is a danger that conditions of exchange fixed by governments will reflect power relations and fail to satisfy all parties. Veblen and the Marxists, struck by the disadvantages of a commercial system to some extent distorted by the capitalists, did not realize that the only alternative to the commercial system was political planning. The industrial system of production does not contain within itself any regulating or distributing mechanism. Such a mechanism is inevitably commercial or political, or rather both, but in unequal proportions.

Veblen and the socialists, when they conceived a situation in which feudalism and capitalism had been abolished, assumed the existence of governments which would express faithfully and with absolute impartiality, the aspirations and interests of the masses. It was assumed that these aspirations were peaceful, that the interests of all nations were in accord, and that free exchange, organized by a supra-national power, would correspond both to men's aspirations and to their interests. This optimistic view failed to recognize what historians, reasoning by analogy, had observed: that industrial society does not exclude authoritarian or despotic régimes.

These despotisms are not and will not be mere temporary survivals of the dynastic state; they reveal one of the permanent possibilities of technical or mass civilization. These despotisms, which profess allegiance to conflicting ideologies, will be arrayed one against the other, each proclaiming peace and democracy as their watchwords. But the peace of one is war in the eyes of the other, and the democracy of one is tyranny to the other. Worse still; the adherence of the masses to these despotisms will perhaps be gained by employing a combination of terror and propaganda. If atomic weapons did not make a major war an act of madness, it is even possible that the masses would follow their despots along the path of conquest. By participating in collective power men find satisfactions which sweep aside economic calculations and make sacrifices meaningful. The desire for power and pride in surpassing other men, are no less profound impulses than the desire for worldly goods. This will to power can be satisfied in and through the community. If power is an end in itself and not just a means, will industry suffice to make peace reign between men who care less about living than ruling?

Let us reiterate briefly the stages of our analysis.

The events of the first half of the century have largely confirmed the prophecies of philosophers who judged the possibilities of the future in terms of what had happened in the past. In retrospect, the last two wars seem to us to be civil wars of the Western Republic; but in the time of the Macedonian hegemony or the Roman Empire the Peloponnesian War must also have looked like a Greek civil war. All wars which preceded the imperial unification of an area of civilization became in retrospect civil wars in the eyes of citizens of the established empire. Probably these are the real wars and the most ruthless. Strangers have no reason to fight; at the very most they kill each other when land or food is lacking. Only crusades or religious wars have the bitterness of civil wars.

Moreover, perhaps the Greeks regretted having broken up the city system by fighting the Peloponnesian War to a finish. No Englishman regrets having paid for resisting Hitler by the break-up of the Empire. One does not like to ask whether a compromise peace concluded in 1916, even if it gave the domination of the continent to Imperial Germany, would not have been preferable to the most costly and sterile of victories.

Neither the survivals of the *ancien régime* in Germany and Japan nor the imperialist conflicts between the European home countries, were the principal causes of the two wars. The spirit of the *ancien régime* has only degenerated into barbarism when revived by the passions of a popular movement. The will to conquer and pride in domination are not a monopoly of the nobility; millions of men may dream of enjoying them by participating in a national community: 'The kneeling slave dreams of ruling the world' (Marquis de Custine).

Waged by nations which wanted to be peaceful and believed themselves to be so, and by soldiers who were only civilians in uniform, the European wars, more than those of any other century, were 'wars to end war', accompanied by a tumult of competing propaganda slogans. Conscript armies, when they ceased to be police forces, became mass armies which could undergo and inflict immense losses, supported by the efforts of entire nations. The characteristic of the second stage of modern civilization which was, according to Comte, the subordination of industry to war and the use of the resources provided by industry for military strength, became the major characteristic of all societies which were, to a greater degree than ever before, military and industrial at the same time. The worker and the soldier: two symbolic figures, complementary and no longer antithetic.

The fact that the European countries were also the possessors of vast empires in Asia and Africa was neither the remote nor the immediate cause of the outbreak. But the European wars assumed a universal dimension and significance because of Europe's place in the world. Indians, Senegalese, Vietnamiens, and Algerians came to fight and to die in Flanders and Lorraine, while Frenchmen, Germans, and Englishmen clashed in equatorial forests or in the deserts of the Near East. Europeans did not fight to the death to share out the world, but because they had fought to the death, together they lost the domination of the world.

The pattern of the European war of 1914–45 may be compared with that of the Peloponnesian War which was divided into two periods by the armistice of Nicias, and it has historical precedents; but the weapons used, the size of the theatre of operations, and the stakes involved in the conflict, give this unique complex of events its specific features. The bi-polar structure of the diplomatic situation in the European–American complex is also not without precedent. The impossibility of peace and the rejection of war is not a radically new phenomenon. Empires—Rome and the Parthians, Byzantium and the Arabs—have coexisted for centuries, not without peripheral conflicts, but without war to the death. Failing a joint domination, the two Great Powers must in reason prefer the limited hazards of an armed peace to the measureless risk of total war.

The present situation has none the less certain new characteristics connected with industrial society. Henceforth the fruits of victory for the Great Powers are derisory in relation to the inevitable cost of the war. The common interest of states possessing atomic weapons in not fighting far outweighs the separate interests which oppose them in this or that area of the world.

The Russo–American rivalry, created by circumstances rather than by men's ambitions or passions, is concerned not with the territory of either of the two states but with the destiny of other nations, old nations of Europe or countries of Africa or Asia previously colonized or dominated. While Europe seems to be the object of Russo–American antagonism, the latter resembles the conflicts which have frequently occurred between two claimants to an empire. But once the U.S.A. and the Soviet Union oppose each other not because the two states want to destroy or enslave each other but because their ideologies are incompatible and the other states too weak to defend themselves alone, the situation becomes unique. Never before has diplomacy been world-wide, as it has been since the second European war, and never before have the two dominant states of an international system competed simultaneously for hegemony over the other parts of the world. The rejection of war is not connected only with the destructive power of nuclear weapons, but also with the purposes of the conflict. Total war between the U.S.A. and the Soviet Union would not settle once and for all the fate of the rest of the world.

The consequences of industrialism are contradictory, some aspects being favourable to war, some to peace. Nuclear weapons make any major war insane and the responsibility for development makes domination costly. But ideological war, to return to Comte's expression, remains possible, since instead of the clash between the *ancien régime* and a new spirit, we see a clash between two versions of the new spirit.

These contradictory aspects of the present situation explain the caution of the prophets. How can one prophesy peace when so many people are committed to violence and when a single atomic war might well render part of the world uninhabitable? How can one prophesy war when the Great Powers have so many motives for fighting and nevertheless refuse to do so? For the next few years one hopes for a limitation of warfare. Further than that, it is impossible to see.

Nevertheless, even beyond this transitional phase, uncertainty remains. What would be required then to confirm the pacific nature of industrial society? The raising of the living standards of the least favoured nations, the slowing down of demographic growth and the acceleration of economic progress, the formation and strengthening of political unities, the appeasement of ideological passions and the acceptance of the partial legitimacy of the various economic and political régimes; these are the conditions, easy to imagine but difficult to realize, in which the spread of industrial society would in theory cease to foster new conflicts as fast as it settles old ones.

Is this theory itself correct? Would men cease to hold exclusive ideologies when there were no longer differences in living standards to conceal? Would men of all races recognize each other's humanity and equality when they effectively shared in the same material civilization?

If one supposes that all the difficulties of the transitional period were surmounted, would industrial society be a permanent source of war or an opportunity for peace? Is industry 'the weapon of a beast of prey', as Spengler said, or an apprenticeship to reason?

It seems to me that the answer is contained in the question. Industrial society *may* teach people to be reasonable if it ceases to be regarded as the instrument of a beast of prey. Comte was wrong to confuse the military spirit with that of a military caste; the disappearance of professional soldiers does not imply the triumph of pacifism. He misjudged the danger of national collisions; the *avant garde* of humanity, against the advice of the founder of positivism, set out to conquer the backward peoples. Whatever the number of Comte's errors or omissions, the same inescapable question remains: has war still a function when there is no longer a military caste, when work is the only source of wealth, when the whole of humanity is united in exploiting natural resources, and when destructive weapons threaten the very basis of civilization? At the present time, small wars may still have a function in the stage when nations are being formed and when there are great disparities in the industrial development of the different countries. The ideological rivalry of the two Great Powers, which is also contemporaneous with the period of transition in which industrial civilization has to coexist with incompatible traditions, may easily transform a local conflict into a total war. At a later stage, when the whole of humanity and not merely a part of it has entered on an era of continuous expansion, why should not the peace which has been achieved by the Western Republic be extended to the rest of humanity?

There is no guarantee that there will be anything beyond what we may, with Comte, call the transitional stage. But if the peoples of Asia within the next hundred years overcame the vicious circle of poverty, if the Soviet states, without giving up a planned economy and the Western states, without abandoning the principle of a pluralist régime, recognized that they constitute species of the same civilization; in other words, if the ideologies were no longer at war, and if all nations were reaping the benefits of productive work, what would be the sense of great wars?

Man has not changed, the psychologist would reply: he remains capable of aggression, he has been and will remain a beast of prey. To be sure; but while individual aggression is perhaps a permanent condition, it is not a sufficient cause of wars and violence between groups. The individual can satisfy his fighting instincts elsewhere than on the battlefield where armies meet. Societies have not changed, the anthropologist would reply; they establish themselves by conflict, and each society consolidates its unity by an image of the world or a system of values which inevitably brings it into conflict with other societies. Millenial religions preach the brotherhood of all men precisely because temporal communities divide humanity. The churches themselves follow a path which leads inevitably to discord although their doctrine knows no frontiers. It may be, indeed, that the antagonism between the earthly city and the city of God, between the Gospel and the Church, will continue for ever. Perhaps human communities are destined to singularity, and in consequence to ethnic conflicts and religious wars. But pacification does not presuppose non-violence and love between nations. Unless the object of the conqueror is the extermination of the vanquished, *reasonable* statesmen, knowing the cost of an industrial war and the necessity for the master to maintain the standard of living of the slave, will prefer peace to military adventures.

Let me repeat: there may be nothing beyond the transitional stage during which the diffusion of industrial society comes up against the resistance of age-old traditions, upsets the stable order of the past, spreads misery among countless multitudes, and increases the causes of conflict. But if there is something beyond, it seems to me that there is no proof that *homo sapiens* must finish his earthly career in an insane catastrophe. The Faustian spirit, we are told, inspires the search for scientific truth, the eagerness to produce, and the will to power. I agree. It was a mistake to believe, as in the nineteenth century, that the domination over nature would rid men of the desire to dominate each other. But is it right to believe that men will be as anxious to dominate when mastery brings nothing but the glory of ruling? It is true that industrial societies are inspired by a passion to know, to possess, and to enjoy. If peace on earth can be based only on detachment and asceticism, modern societies are certainly farther from it than any in the past. But the attempts to bring about peace by changing men's hearts have all failed. The endeavour to which humanity is condemned today is without precedent. The transformation of all men into workers, all workers into citizens, and all citizens into members of a universal community of labour; this is the meaning of the industrial society which Comte imagined.

Comte certainly did not foresee, nor would he have approved, the unbridled and unqualified technological progress which forces men to choose between collective suicide and peace. In his view, the essence of industrial society was not the power to produce or to destroy, but the extinction of the military caste and the pre-eminence of work. He dreamed of restoring social stability by the permanence of a true doctrine, of offering men the prospect of constantly increasing wealth, but also of a perpetual re-adaptation to an unpredictable technology.

If Comte's theory is treated as a prophecy, then it is reasonable to dismiss ironically the teaching of a man who declared inevitable a future which has not come to pass. But neither Comte, nor for that matter Marx, is one of those philosophers who were condemned by Sir Isaiah Berlin in a previous 'Auguste Comte Memorial Lecture', and who seek in an allegedly inevitable future an excuse for their own resignation.

Neither Comte nor Marx claimed to justify the unjustifiable by declaring it to be inevitable. The chief fault of both is optimism. They assumed, implicitly or explicitly, that phenomena which no longer have any meaning or function necessarily disappear. They did not conceive that the absurd might survive (although Marx's well-known formula, 'socialism or barbarism', suggests such an eventuality). Marx predicted socialism in order to encourage the proletariat in the revolutionary action which he believed to be necessary for the good of humanity. Comte predicted the coming of a positivist society in order to make men conscious of what was required for the stability of industrial civilization. The enunciation of an inevitable future emerges, in one case as an appeal to action, in the other as an appeal to moral responsibility.

Comte's appeal to moral responsibility takes on an added significance in present circumstances. Technological progress ends, not by accident but by a logical development, in giving men the power to destroy themselves. Man has always had the means to kill his fellow man. With hydrogen bombs and rockets, societies have the means to make the world uninhabitable.

Comte was wrong to believe that wars would no longer occur because they would have no function. But should we be justified in going to the other extreme and seeing no difference between what is sensible and what is insane, between the reasonable and the absurd? Should we be right to maintain that universal catastrophe is as probable as salvation? Those who confine their hopes to this world cannot but choose the universal community of work, which those whom we call optimists dreamed of in the last century. Today we are more aware of the sacrifices it involves, of its improbability in the short run, and yet, in spite of everything, the remote possibility of achieving it.

We have lost our taste for prophecies; let us not forget the duty of hope.

A Note on Veblen and Schumpeter

The theories of Veblen and Schumpeter are similar in several respects. They had, almost simultaneously, the same fundamental idea. Imperialism and militarism are survivals of feudal civilization and are contrary to the spirit and essence of industrial society. Veblen's theory is set out in his book, *Imperial Germany and the Industrial Revolution*, which was published in 1915, and that of Schumpeter in his long essay, 'Zur Sociologie der Imperialismen', published in 1919 in the *Archiv für Sozialwissenschaft und Sozialpolitik*.[1] Besides their central thesis, the two theories have in common a comparison between the cases of England and Germany. Both authors thought the case of England was *normal* and that of Germany *abnormal*. In the long run, the imperialist attitude, the will to conquer for the sake of conquest, and the will to power for the sake of power, seemed to them incompatible with the interests and ways of thought which the diffusion of the industrial system would spread among the masses.

Veblen and Schumpeter also analysed in similar terms the

[1] English translation in J. A. Schumpeter, *Imperialism and Social Classes* (Oxford, 1951).

interweaving of capitalism and imperialism, or in other words, the solidarity which is gradually created between the nobility (or the military caste) and industrial and commercial interests. Veblen denounced commercialized nationalism, and Schumpeter analysed the mechanism by which cartels and trusts, limiting sales at home by maintaining high prices, are obliged to sell abroad at dumping prices. The whole apparatus of protection of the national market and aggressive exports pushes capitalism towards a foreign policy of expansion and, finally, of conquest. Moreover, Schumpeter showed how the *bourgeoisie*, caught between the proletariat and the aristocracy, allows the latter to impose on it aristocratic values and attitudes.

The bourgeoisie seeks to win over the state for itself and in return serves the state and state interests that are different from its own. Imbued with the spirit of the old autocracy, trained by it, the bourgeoisie often takes over its ideology, even where, as in France, the sovereign is eliminated and the official power of the nobility has been broken. Because the sovereign needed soldiers, the modern bourgeois —at least in his slogans—is an even more vehement advocate of an increasing population. Because the sovereign was in a position to exploit conquests, needed them to be a victorious warlord, the bourgeoisie thirsts for national glory—even in France, worshipping a headless body, as it were. Because the sovereign found a large gold hoard useful, the bourgeoisie even today cannot be swerved from its bullionist prejudices. Because the autocratic state paid attention to the trader and manufacturer chiefly as the most important sources of taxes and credits, today even the intellectual who has not a shred of property looks on international commerce, not from the viewpoint of the consumer, but from that of the trader and exporter. Because pugnacious sovereigns stood in constant fear of attack by their equally pugnacious neighbours, the modern bourgeois attribute aggressive designs to neighbouring peoples. All such modes of thought are essentially noncapitalist. Indeed, they vanish most quickly wherever capitalism fully prevails. They are survivals of the autocratic alignment of interests, and they endure wherever the autocratic state endures on the old basis and with the old orientation, even though more and more democratized and otherwise transformed. They bear witness to the extent to which essentially imperialist absolutism has patterned not only the economy of the bourgeoisie but also its mind—in the interests of autocracy and against those of the bourgeoisie itself. (*Imperialism and Social Classes*, p. 124.)

And again:

Nationalism and militarism, while not creatures of capitalism, become 'capitalized' and in the end draw their best energies from capitalism. Capitalism involves them in its workings and thereby keeps them alive, politically as well as economically. And they, in turn, affect capitalism, cause it to deviate from the course it might have followed alone, support many of its interests. (Ibid., p. 128.)

This theory leads both authors to predict the decline of imperialism and of militarism. At the end of his essay in 1919, Schumpeter did in fact predict that sooner or later imperialism was doomed, because it was foreign to the spirit of modern civilization. Veblen made the same prediction about Japan. However, both, for different reasons, were less confident than Comte in their optimism.

Veblen was as hostile to the market economy as he was to classical or marginalist economic theory. Commercialized nationalism seemed to him the inevitable result of a commercial and financial system which was superimposed on the system of production, and entirely governed by the pursuit of profit. He apparently conceived a peaceful industrial system as non-competitive, democratic and non-commercial, managerial and supra-national. Violently hostile to Imperial Germany, Veblen denounced the armistice of 1918, which saved the dynastic state and the old style of diplomatic relations. He sympathized at first with the Bolshevik revolution. The league of peaceful states which he conceived for the maintenance of peace, presupposed that the rivalries between sovereign states would be surmounted, and it implied governments capable of organizing the industrial system on a supranational basis, providing justice for all.

In a book published at the beginning of 1917, *An Inquiry into the Nature of Peace and the Terms of its Perpetuation*, Veblen presents not only aggressive nationalism but even patriotism as a survival of the feudal spirit or the dynastic state. 'The nation, without the bond of dynastic loyalty, is after all a make-shift idea, an episodic half-way station in the sequence' (p. 140). At the same time, he predicted that if Germany and Japan retained the institutions of the dynastic state, they would wage a war of aggression before the industrial system had sufficiently destroyed the old spirit of obedience, sacrifice, respect, and fidelity. Finally, he thought that commercial interests, fearing a revolution, would foster nationalistic envy and rivalry.

Schumpeter, on the other hand, believed that the market economy and economic calculation were foreign to nationalism and imperialism so long as they were not distorted by monopoly capitalism allied with the pre-industrial classes. In the long run, this alliance would be undermined by the development of industrial society. But Schumpeter seems to have had increasing doubts about explaining imperialism exclusively in terms of survivals of the past. The will to conquer is irrational from the point of view of the economic interests of the masses; nevertheless it may survive the development of capitalism if it is inspired by human passions and if the managerial classes, which have been recruited from the people, adopt the attitude of aristocratic or military castes.